OUR CHANGING PLANET

Habitat Loss

Lucy Bashford

Explore other books at:
WWW.ENGAGEBOOKS.COM

VANCOUVER, B.C.

→ WWW.ENGAGEBOOKS.COM

Habitat Loss - Our Changing Planet: *Level 3*
Bashford, Lucy 1958 –
Text © 2023 Engage Books
Design © 2023 Engage Books

Edited by: A.R. Roumanis, Ashley Lee,
Melody Sun & Sarah Harvey
Design by: Mandy Christiansen

Text set in Montserrat Regular.
Chapter headings set in Animated Gothic Light.

FIRST EDITION / FIRST PRINTING

LIBRARY AND ARCHIVES CANADA CATALOGUING IN PUBLICATION

Title: Habitat Loss / Lucy Bashford.
Names: Bashford, Lucy, author.
Description: Series statement: Our changing planet

Identifiers: Canadiana (print) 20230447783 | Canadiana (ebook) 20230447791
ISBN 978-1-77476-903-4 (hardcover)
ISBN 978-1-77476-904-1 (softcover)
ISBN 978-1-77476-905-8 (epub)
ISBN 978-1-77476-906-5 (pdf)
ISBN 978-1-77878-124-7 (audio)

Subjects:
LCSH: Habitat (Ecology)—Juvenile literature.
LCSH: Habitat conservation—Juvenile literature.
LCSH: Nature—Effect of human beings on—Juvenile literature.

Classification: LCC QH541.14 .B37 2023 | DDC J577—DC23

This project has been made possible in part by the Government of Canada.

Canada

Contents

4 What Is Habitat Loss?

6 A Closer Look

8 Causes of Habitat Loss 1

10 Causes of Habitat Loss 2

12 Habitat Loss and Climate Change

14 Effects on the Planet

16 Effects on Humans

18 Habitat Loss Around the World 1

20 Habitat Loss Around the World 2

22 Habitat Loss Solutions 1

24 Habitat Loss Solutions 2

26 The Helpers

28 How Can You Help?

30 Quiz

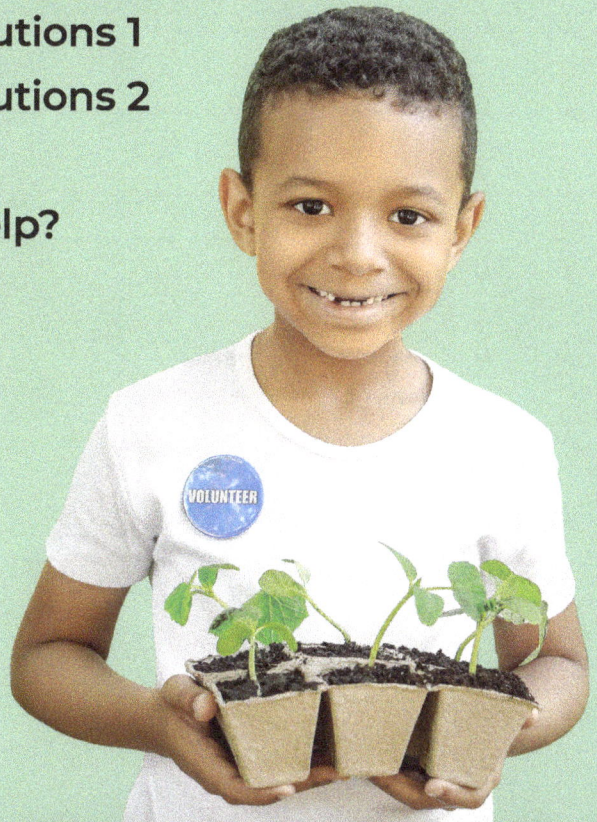

What Is Habitat Loss?

A habitat is a natural place where plants and animals live. It is part of an **ecosystem**. Habitat loss is when a habitat is destroyed or damaged. Plants and animals lose their homes.

KEY WORD

Ecosystem: a community of living and nonliving things that work together to stay healthy.

Habitat Loss can be reversed. This means a habitat can go back to the way it was before it was damaged. Many habitats cannot do this on their own. They need people to help them.

People often plant trees or clean up garbage to help reverse habitat loss.

A Closer Look

There are three main kinds of habitat loss. Habitat destruction is when a habitat is damaged so badly that it can no longer support life. Plants and some animals die. Other animals have to find somewhere else to live.

Habitat degradation is when the health of a habitat is made worse. Plants and animals get sick or die. Habitat fragmentation is when a habitat is split into smaller pieces. Animals cannot move around as freely as they once could.

Causes of Habitat Loss 1

Habitat loss from human activity can last forever. One of the major causes of habitat loss is deforestation. This is when people cut down trees to make room for things like farms, towns, or roads.

In South America, forests are burned to create farmland for cows.

All kinds of pollution made by humans can harm habitats. Garbage can **smother** plants or make animals sick if they try to eat it. Chemicals used on farms to make plants grow often get washed into habitats by the rain. Too much of these chemicals can kill plants.

KEY WORD

Smother: cover something and stop it from breathing.

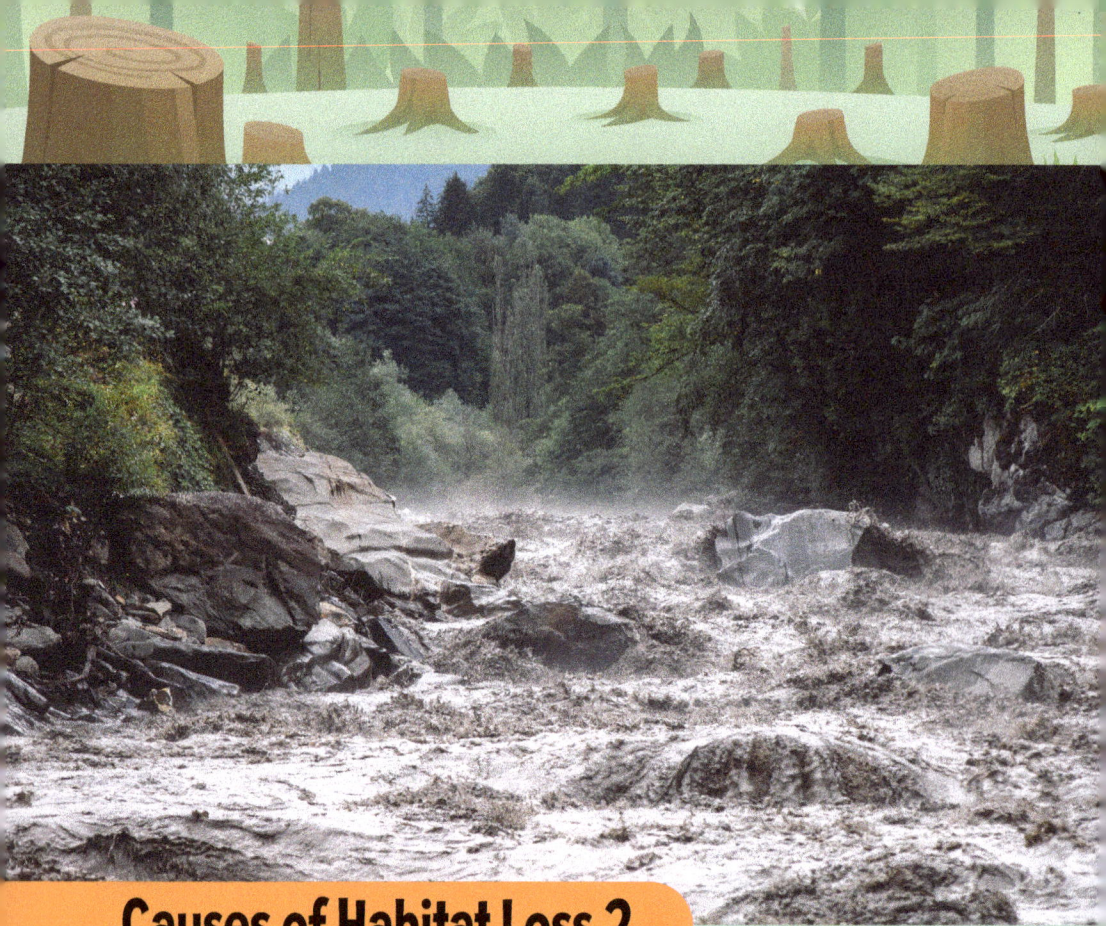

Causes of Habitat Loss 2

Habitat loss is sometimes caused by natural disasters. Tornadoes can rip trees out of the ground. Many **species** may die in a flood.

KEY WORD

Species: a group of similar animals or plants that can make babies with each other.

Habitat loss from natural causes often does not last long. A large wildfire can destroy an entire species in an area. But different plants and animals might move in after the fire.

Almost 70,000 wildfires were reported in the US in 2022.

Habitat Loss and Climate Change

Climate change is a change in the average temperature over a long period of time. It is getting worse because of human activity. When people drive cars or use electricity, gas gets released into the air. This gas slowly warms Earth.

Climate change is causing more natural disasters. Warmer temperatures can lead to more wildfires. **Glaciers** melting in hot weather can cause floods. More natural disasters means more habitat loss.

KEY WORD

Glaciers: huge masses of ice that form over many years.

Effects on the Planet

Habitat loss can cause biodiversity loss. Biodiversity means the different kinds of life that live in an area. It helps keep ecosystems healthy. Healthy ecosystems provide more food for animals and are able to heal faster after disasters.

Habitat loss has caused many plants and animals to become endangered. This means they are at risk of dying out forever. Some plants and animals have already gone **extinct**.

Extinct: when an animal population stops existing.

More than 150,000 species were listed as endangered by the International Union for Conservation of Nature in 2022.

Effects on Humans

Habitats give people clean air, water, and food. Scientists use some plants and animals to make medicines. When habitats are destroyed, there are less of these things for people to use.

Yew trees are the source of a drug that fights cancer. They are likely to become endangered soon.

Some animals try to stay in their habitat even after humans have taken over. This means humans and wild animals live closer to each other. When wild animals get close to humans, they can give them diseases.

Habitat Loss Around the World 1

In Southeast Asia, rainforests are cut down to make farms for oil palm trees. This is destroying the habitats of many animals that are already endangered. Orangutans, pygmy elephants, and Sumatran rhinos have fewer places to live as oil palm tree farms grow.

Palm oil is used in many human foods as well as things like shampoo and toothpaste.

Pollution created by humans is one of the reasons the Caribbean coral reefs are dying. Coral reefs are ecosystems where lots of sea life live. They are made up of sea creatures called corals. Without these coral reefs, sea creatures lose their homes and their source of food.

Habitat Loss Around the World 2

In 2019 and 2021, more than 20 percent of Australia's forests were destroyed by wildfire. It was caused by high temperatures and a long **drought**. About three billion animals were killed or had to find new homes.

KEY WORD

Drought: a long period without rain.

Jaguars used to live between the American Southwest and northern Argentina. About half of their habitat has been destroyed to make way for cow farms. Most jaguars live in the Amazon rainforest now.

Habitat Loss Solutions 1

Protected areas are places where governments have **banned** most or all human activities. This helps keep the habitats in these areas safe. Many protected areas are parks people can visit to enjoy nature.

KEY WORD

Banned: stopped something from happening.

People are building wildlife corridors to connect fragmented habitats. These are strips of land built over or under areas that have been taken over by humans. They allow animals to safely move from one part of a habitat to another.

Habitat Loss Solutions 2

Some farmers are learning to grow food with less dangerous chemicals to help keep habitats safe. The food they grow is called organic food. More and more people are buying organic food and supporting these farmers.

People around the world are joining the zero waste movement. They are trying to create as little garbage in their daily lives as possible. There are even zero waste stores where people can bring their own containers to fill instead of buying food in packages.

The Helpers

The World Wide Fund for Nature (WWF) works to protect wild animals and the places they live. They help restore habitats that have been damaged. They also protect habitats and teach communities how to live without damaging nature.

The WWF is one of the largest companies in the world that protects nature.

The Nature Conservancy protects habitats all over the world. They work with governments and communities to come up with ways to keep habitats safe and healthy. They help create protected areas where little human activity is allowed.

The Nature Conservancy does work in more than 70 countries and territories.

How Can You Help?

Visit national parks or wildlife sanctuaries. These are areas where plants and animals are protected. Going to them helps keep them open.

Leave things the way you found them. Moving rocks at the ocean to look for crabs or moving a log in the forest to find a frog can be fun. But these are homes for lots of animals, so make sure to put them back when you are done.

Quiz

Test your knowledge of habitat loss by answering the following questions. The questions are based on what you have read in this book. The answers are listed on the bottom of the next page.

1 What is a habitat?

2 What is one of the major causes of habitat loss?

3 How many wildfires were reported in the US in 2022.

4 What is biodiversity?

5 What kind of trees are the source of a drug that fights cancer?

What are coral reefs?

Explore Other Level 3 Readers.

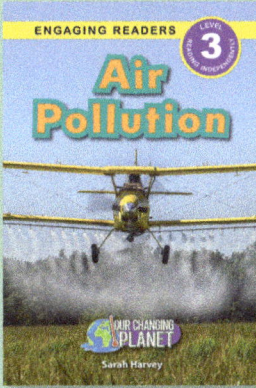

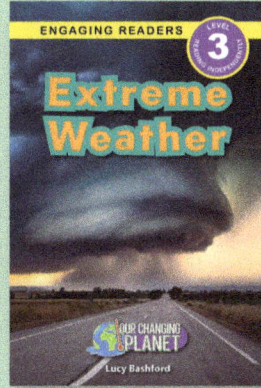

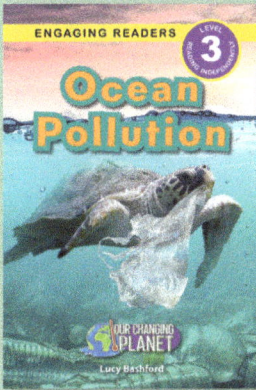

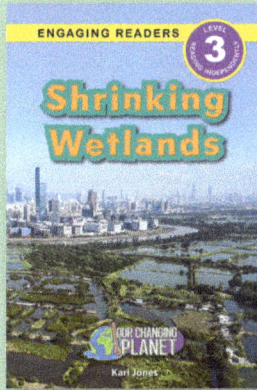

ENGAGING READERS · LEVEL 3 · READING INDEPENDENCE
Air Pollution
OUR CHANGING PLANET
Sarah Harvey

ENGAGING READERS · LEVEL 3 · READING INDEPENDENCE
Climate Change
OUR CHANGING PLANET
Sarah Harvey

ENGAGING READERS · LEVEL 3 · READING INDEPENDENCE
Extreme Weather
OUR CHANGING PLANET
Lucy Bashford

ENGAGING READERS · LEVEL 3 · READING INDEPENDENCE
Ocean Pollution
OUR CHANGING PLANET
Lucy Bashford

ENGAGING READERS · LEVEL 3 · READING INDEPENDENCE
Shrinking Wetlands
OUR CHANGING PLANET
Karl Jones

ENGAGING READERS · LEVEL 3 · READING INDEPENDENCE
Diabetes
UNDERSTANDING Mind and Body
Kit Caudron-Robinson

ENGAGING READERS · LEVEL 3 · READING INDEPENDENCE
Obesity
UNDERSTANDING Mind and Body
Kit Caudron-Robinson

ENGAGING READERS · LEVEL 3 · READING INDEPENDENCE
Autism
UNDERSTANDING Mind and Body
AJ Knight

ENGAGING READERS · LEVEL 3 · READING INDEPENDENCE
Vision Loss
UNDERSTANDING Mind and Body
Hannalora Leavitt & Sarah Harvey

Visit www.engagebooks.com/readers

Answers:
1. A natural place where plants and animals live 2. Deforestation
3. Almost 70,000 4. The different kinds of life that live in an area
5. Yew trees 6. Ecosystems where lots of sea life live

www.ingramcontent.com/pod-product-compliance
Lightning Source LLC
Chambersburg PA
CBHW040227040426
42331CB00039B/3408